Healthy Eating

Vegetables

Nancy Dickmann

Heinemann Library
Chicago, Illinois

S0-ADE-764

www.heinemannraintree.com

Visit our website to find out more information about Heinemann-Raintree books.

To order:

☎ Phone 888-454-2279

💻 Visit www.heinemannraintree.com to browse our catalog and order online.

©2010 Heinemann Library
an imprint of Capstone Global Library, LLC
Chicago, Illinois

All rights reserved. No part of this publication may be reproduced or transmitted in any form or by any means, electronic or mechanical, including photocopying, recording, taping, or any information storage and retrieval system, without permission in writing from the publisher.

Edited by Siân Smith, Nancy Dickmann, and Rebecca Rissman
Designed by Joanna Hinton-Malivoire
Picture research by Elizabeth Alexander
Production by Victoria Fitzgerald
Originated by Capstone Global Library Ltd
Printed and bound in China by South China Printing Company Ltd

ISBN 978-1-4329-3979-3
14 13 12 11 10
10 9 8 7 6 5 4 3 2 1

Library of Congress Cataloging-in-Publication Data
Dickmann, Nancy.
  Vegetables / Nancy Dickmann.
    p. cm. -- (Healthy eating)
  Includes bibliographical references and index.
  ISBN 978-1-4329-3979-3 (hc) -- ISBN 978-1-4329-3986-1 (pb) 1. Vegetables in human nutrition--Juvenile literature. I. Title.
  QP144.V44D53 2011
  613.2--dc22

                    2009045480

Acknowledgements
We would like to thank the following for permission to reproduce photographs: © Capstone Publishers pp.**16**, **22** (Karon Dubke); Alamy pp.**20**, **23 middle** (© MBI); Corbis pp.**10** (© amanaimages), **21** (© Gideon Mendel); Getty Images p.**17** (Robert Daly/OJO Images); iStockphoto pp.**4**, **23 bottom** (© Dana Bartekoske), **7** (© David T. Gomez), **8** (© Shane Cummins), **11** (© Jon Faulknor), **14** (© Doug Schneider), **15** (© Francisco Romero), **23 top** (© Mark Hatfield); Photolibrary pp.**5** (Image Source), **6** (Mode Images), **12** (OJO Images/Andrew Olney), **13** (Jasper James); Shutterstock pp.**9** (© Elena Kalistratova), **18** (© Monkey Business Images); USDA Center for Nutrition Policy and Promotion p.**19**.

Front cover photograph of vegetables reproduced with permission of © Capstone Publishers (Karon Dubke). Back cover photograph reproduced with permission of iStockphoto (© Doug Schneider).

We would like to thank Dr Sarah Schenker for her invaluable help in the preparation of this book.

Every effort has been made to contact copyright holders of material reproduced in this book. Any omissions will be rectified in subsequent printings if notice is given to the publishers.

Contents

R0431467653

What Are Vegetables?

A vegetable is a type of plant we eat.

Eating vegetables can keep
us healthy.

carrot

Some vegetables grow under the ground.

peas

Some vegetables grow above the ground.

Looking at Vegetables

onion

Some vegetables are short
and round.

bean

Some vegetables are long and thin.

Many vegetables are green.

beet

carrot

Some vegetables are orange
or purple.

How Vegetables Help Us

Vegetables are full of nutrients.

You need nutrients to stay healthy.

Eating carrots helps keep your skin
and eyes healthy.

Eating spinach helps keep your blood healthy.

Eating sweet potatoes gives you energy.

You need energy to work and play.

Healthy Eating

We need to eat five servings of fruit and vegetables each day.

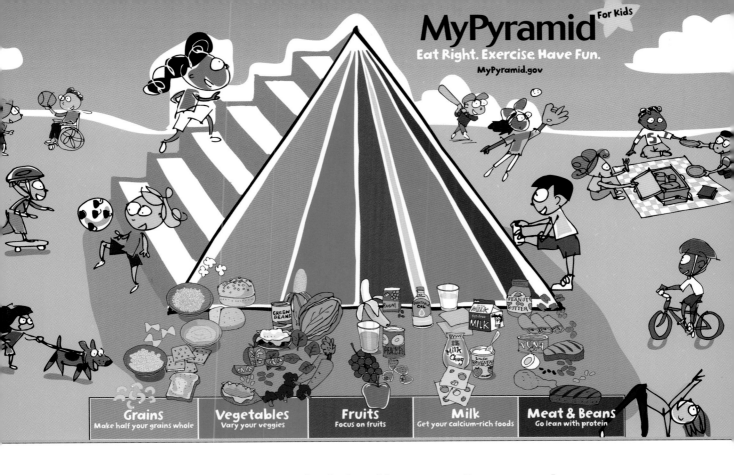

The food pyramid tells us to eat foods from each food group.

We eat vegetables to stay healthy.

We eat vegetables because they taste good!

Find the Vegetables

Here is a healthy dinner. Can you find two vegetables?

Answer on page 24

Picture Glossary

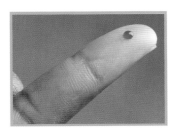 **blood** red liquid inside your body. Blood takes food and air to all your body parts.

 **energy** the power to do something. We need energy when we work or play.

 **nutrients** things our bodies need to stay healthy. You can get nutrients in different foods.

Index

Answer to quiz on page 22: The two vegetables are carrots and broccoli.

Notes for parents and teachers

Before reading

Explain that we need to eat a range of different foods to stay healthy. Splitting foods into different groups can help us understand how much food we should eat from each group. Introduce the vegetables group. How many different vegetables can the children think of? Explain that eating five portions of vegetables every day can help us to stay healthy.

After reading

- Choose children to mime some benefits of eating vegetables for the others to guess. These can include keeping our skin, teeth, and gums health, building strong muscles, healing cuts and bruises, fighting illnesses, helping us see in the dark, helping us to digest food and get rid of waste products.

- Create a bar chart or pictogram with the children to show the different vegetables they have eaten or tasted over the course of a week. Make it a challenge to see how high you can get the bar for each vegetable to go, and to see how many new vegetables can be added to the chart.

- Ask the children to bring in pictures of as many different vegetables as they can find. Divide the children into groups and ask the groups to explore different ways of sorting the vegetables. For example, they might sort them by shape, size, color, preference, or whether they can be eaten raw. Collages of grouped vegetables can be put up on the wall.